Albania

by Corey Anderson

Consultant: Marjorie Faulstich Orellana, PhD
Professor of Urban Schooling
University of California, Los Angeles

New York, New York

Credits

Cover, © brusinski/iStock and © alsem/iStock; 3, © Jasius/Getty Images; 4, © EyeEm/Getty Images; 5T, © iStockphoto/Getty Images; 5B, © Ligak/Shutterstock; 6, © Minestrone/Wikimedia; 7, © master2/iStock; 8–9, © Westend61/Getty Images; 8B, © corgarashu/Shutterstock; 9B, © iStockphoto/Getty Images; 10T, © Michal Blaho/Shutterstock; 10B, © Jasius/Getty Images; 11, © Sergey Uryadnikov/Shutterstock; 12B, © imageBROKER RF/Getty Images; 12–13, © Gert Olsson/Shutterstock; 13B, © Kutay Tanir/Getty Images; 14, © Enea Kelo/Shutterstock; 15, © Dinosmichail/Dreamstime; 16, © iStockphoto/Getty Images; 17T, © U.S. Department of State/Wikimedia; 17B, © Ligak/Shutterstock; 18T, © Jess Kraft/Shutterstock; 18B, © Artur Widak/NurPhoto/ZUMA Press/Newscom; 19, © Zvonimir Atletic/Shutterstock; 20T, © Jasmin Merdan/Getty Images; 20B, © milosk50/Shutterstock; 21, © Adrian Wojcik/Getty Images; 22, © Brilliant Eye/Shutterstock; 23T, © iStockphoto/Getty Images; 23B, © 500px Unreleased/Getty Images; 24, © suzyco/Getty Images; 25, © DVrcan/Getty Images; 26, © Fanfo/Shutterstock; 27T, © agrofruti/Shutterstock; 27B, © Violetamyftari/Wikimedia; 28–29, © Michael Steele/Getty Images; 29, © Michael Steele/Getty Images; 30M, © Adriana Iacob/Shutterstock; 30B, © EyeEm/Getty Images; 31 (T to B), © Gosiek-B/Getty Images, © Westend61/Getty Images, © ollirg/Getty Images, © iStockphoto/Getty Images, © 500px Prime/Getty Images, and © iStockphoto/Getty Images; 32, © Boris15/Shutterstock.

Publisher: Kenn Goin
Senior Editor: Joyce Tavolacci
Creative Director: Spencer Brinker
Design: Debrah Kaiser
Photo Researcher: Book Buddy Media

Library of Congress Cataloging-in-Publication Data

Names: Anderson, Corey, author.
Title: Albania / by Corey Anderson.
Description: New York, New York : Bearport Publishing, [2020] | Series:
  Countries we come from | Includes bibliographical references and index. |
Identifiers: LCCN 2019010082 (print) | LCCN 2019010402 (ebook) | ISBN
  9781642805819 (ebook) | ISBN 9781642805277 (library binding)
Subjects: LCSH: Albania—Juvenile literature.
Classification: LCC DR943 (ebook) | LCC DR943 .A55 2020 (print) | DDC
  949.65—dc23
LC record available at https://lccn.loc.gov/2019010082

For more information, write to Bearport Publishing Company, Inc., 45 West 21st Street, Suite 3B, New York, New York 10010. Printed in the United States of America.

10 9 8 7 6 5 4 3 2 1

Contents

This Is Albania

Friendly

ANCIENT

Colorful

Albania is a small country in southern Europe.

It borders the Adriatic Sea.

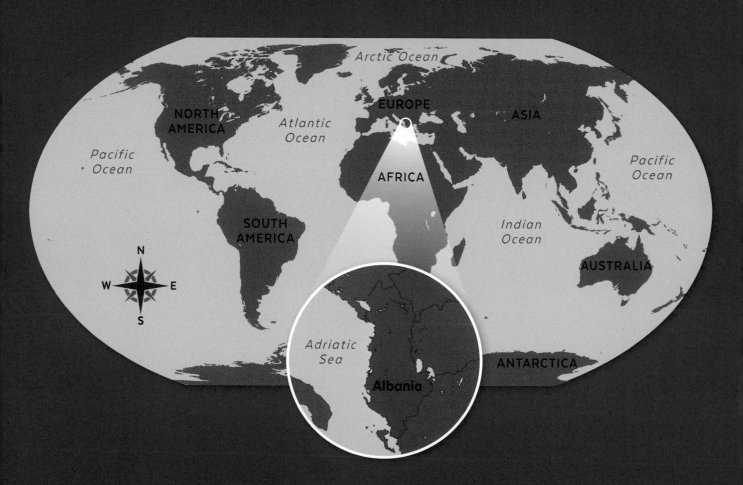

About three million people live in Albania.

Albania has beautiful beaches, forests, and mountains.

Mount Korab is the country's tallest mountain.

Mount Korab

Sparkling blue lakes and rivers cover the land.

Over 3,000 types of plants grow in Albania!

9

Incredible animals live in Albania.

Chamois (SHAM-wah) dart across mountains.

Rare lynxes hunt in forests.

chamois

Albania is home to 140 different types of butterflies!

Eagles soar through the sky.

white-tailed eagle

People have lived in Albania for over 4,000 years!

During that time, different groups were in power, including the Greeks and Ottomans.

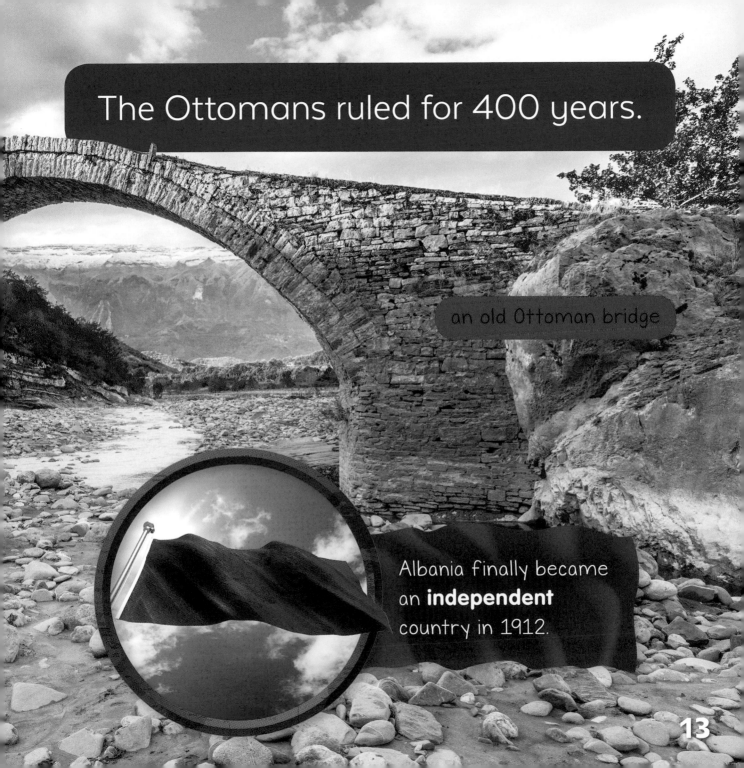

The Ottomans ruled for 400 years.

an old Ottoman bridge

Albania finally became an **independent** country in 1912.

Butrint is an **ancient** city in Albania.

Greeks lived there over 2,000 years ago.

Butrint attracts as many as 1,500 visitors per day!

The Greeks built a huge theater and other buildings.

theater

Albania's colorful **capital** is Tirana.

In 2000, an artist named Edi Rama became Tirana's mayor.

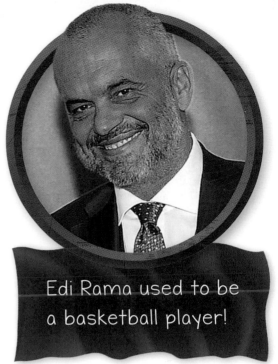

Edi Rama used to be a basketball player!

He painted buildings in bold colors.

Albania is known for its lively folk dancing.

Opinga (ah-PING-gah) are **traditional** Albanian shoes. Many have pom-poms on the toes!

People dance in circles and wave scarves.

About 57 percent of Albanians are Muslim.

mosque

Muslims practice a religion called Islam. They often worship in mosques.

Many Albanians celebrate Eid al-Adha (EED ahl-AH-duh).

This holiday celebrates forgiveness and unity.

21

Albanian is the country's main language.

This language is also called *Shqip* (SHEEP).

This is how you say *hello* in Albanian:

Tungjatjeta (TOON-jaht-YEH-tah)

Shqip is thought to come from the Albanian word for "eagle." Eagles are a common symbol in Albania.

23

Every evening in Albania, people go outside for a walk.

This **custom** is called *xhiro* (JEE-roh).

During xhiro, people walk and talk until nighttime!

stuffed doll

Some Albanians hang stuffed dolls outside their homes. They do this to keep bad luck away!

Food in Albania is rich and tasty.

A very popular dish is *tavë kosi* (TAV KOH-see).

It's made with lamb, rice, and yogurt.

tavë kosi

Albanians also love fresh fruits and vegetables.

A common sweet treat is *flija* (FLEE-uh). It's a cake often served with honey.

Albanians enjoy soccer!

Both children and adults play the game.

Who will score the first goal?

Judo and table tennis are also popular sports in Albania.

Fast Facts

Capital city: Tirana

Population of Albania: About three million

Main language: Albanian, or Shqip

Money: Albanian lek

Major religion: Islam

Neighboring countries include: Greece, Italy, Kosovo, Macedonia, and Montenegro

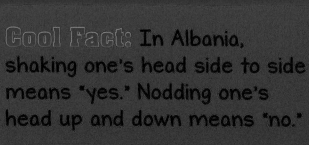

Cool Fact: In Albania, shaking one's head side to side means "yes." Nodding one's head up and down means "no."

ancient (AYN-shunt) very old

capital (KAP-uh-tuhl) the city where a country's government is based

custom (KUSS-tum) a usual way of doing something

independent (in-di-PEN-duhnt) free of control by others

rare (RAIR) not often seen or found

traditional (truh-DISH-uhn-uhl) done a certain way for a long time

Index

Read More

Knowlton, Mary Lee. *Albania (Cultures of the World).* New York: Benchmark (2005).

Mara, Wil. *Albania (Enchantment of the World).* New York: Children's Press (2018).

Learn More Online

To learn more about Albania, visit
www.bearportpublishing.com/CountriesWeComeFrom

About the Author

Corey Anderson is a writer from Los Angeles who loves exploring destinations near and far with her husband, Josh, and sons, Leo and Dane.